BEFORE WE DROWN IN COMMUNICATION

WE MUST LEARN TO SURF.

For today's knowledge workers, life revolves around the inflow and outflow of communication. It comes through more channels than ever: Meetings, conference calls, email, text, voicemail, chat, social media and more. It also comes more frequently than ever — and, often outside of traditional work hours.

Technology has given us new and better ways to connect — but, do we have the right systems to manage it?

In Greek mythology, Sisyphus was condemned by the gods to suffer the worst punishment imaginable: To spend eternity rolling a giant boulder up a steep mountain, only to have the boulder roll back down after the apex was reached — once the boulder hit bottom, the task would repeat again.

Today's knowledge workers face their own modern version of torment- we spend countless hours getting through our in-box, day after day after day. It's overwhelming.

In the end we are left with the feeling that we are never caught up. In fact, after accounting for time spent sitting in meetings, processing emails, and dealing with interruptions, the average worker spends less than half of their time on primary job duties.[1]

We are trapped in the thick of thinning things.

THIS BOOK WAS CREATED
TO HELP YOU BREAK OUT.

[1]Workfront. 2015. *The State of Enterprise Work.*

In the self-improvement industry, much emphasis is placed upon improving individual ability to focus attention, process and set priorities. These are important, even essential skills. Yet, even productivity masters get copied on unnecessary emails and stuck in redundant meetings. They are highly productive at the personal level, but mired in inefficiency at the interpersonal level.

Significant productivity gains are left on the table by teams and organizations that haven't thought about their communication cultures.

Without a consciously designed system in place, individuals devolve into habits that require the least individual effort. For example, rather than identifying the key points of an email (or, considering who really needs to see the key points), many people will spew a block of text and copy everyone. However, what's easiest for the individual ends up being hardest on the team.

It's time to end the madness of our in-box, the endless meetings, the droning conference calls, the death by PowerPoint.

IT'S TIME TO STREAMLINE
OUR WORLD OF WORK.

SAID & DONE

JASON FRANZEN
STEPHAN MARDYKS

Written by Jason Franzen & Stephan Mardyks

Designed by Jason Franzen

Edited by Joseph Alan Wachs

Published by Streamline Certified | Dallas, Texas USA

©2016 Streamline Certified | All rights reserved

ISBN 978-099814241-8

Printed in the United States of America

First Edition

For ordering information, visit:

StreamlineCertified.com/orders

Simplicity is the ultimate sophistication.

- LEONARDO DA VINCI

ONE

TWO

FOREWORD

Though I've spent decades in a career exploring and teaching how to get things done with less effort, reading this book heightened my perspectives and sharpened my focus in that arena even more. And I found it particularly valuable because it applies sophisticated simplicity to how we communicate – a universal experience astoundingly rich in potential but fraught with unproductive practices.

I know the cleaner and clearer our heads are, the more creatively engaged we become in whatever we are doing. This is a very cool handbook for applying that principle to one of the most important aspects of our lives.

Though I've been writing e-mails since 1983, a few minutes after reading this I wrote a much better one.

David Allen
Author of *Getting Things Done*

"When all is said and done,

more is said than done."

- **AESOP**

ONE

PERSPECTIVE

LESS IS MORE

EFFECTIVE

"LESS IS MORE."

Ludwig Mies van der Rohe, 1947
Architect and furniture designer describing minimalism

LESS IS MORE

In this bold statement, the world-renowned architect Mies van der Rohe made the case for achieving more impact through intentionally less decoration in modern architecture. His premise holds true for modern communication.

As the speed and intensity of communication has grown exponentially in the past decades, our attention has been divided and fragmented while messages have overlapped and become mixed together into a dense blur. The mantra has for too long been **MORE** and **FASTER**.

For communication to get our attention in today's world, it must stand out and be unique. Saying less is one of the most powerful ways to do that.

While getting attention is an important step, it is not the ultimate goal. The aim of our communication should be to make an impact — to move ideas forward through action. This is where LESS truly becomes MORE EFFECTIVE.

When we streamline our communication to focus on an essential audience, message, and action, we are creating a clear path for our ideas to reach their objective.

STREAMLINED COMMUNICATION
REQUIRES LESS ENERGY TO SEND IDEAS
FURTHER, FASTER.

"I WOULD HAVE WRITTEN A SHORTER LETTER,
BUT I DID NOT HAVE THE TIME."

Blaise Pascal, 1656
philosopher & scientist

The eloquent self-criticism by the 17th-century French philosopher noted on the opposite page alludes to a key aspect of efficient and effective communication: Clarity takes time and work. The idea of writing a shorter letter by investing more time is a critical concept that we often bypass in the interest of speed.

It is far easier to project a lot of words and string together thoughts as they come to mind than to carefully compose, refine, and edit what we say. Yet, these very acts of refinement are what bring clarity and effectiveness to our communication.

ONLY WHEN WE COMMIT THE TIME AND ATTENTION OUR COMMUNICATION DESERVES CAN WE EXPECT OTHERS TO DO THE SAME.

To streamline communication, we must commit the time and attention required to elevate the quality — above quantity.

THE PARADOX OF MORE

Our instincts tell us: If we want more of something, we must do more of something else.

Work harder to get more done.
Share more of ourselves to learn more of others.
Work more to make more money.

The truth is, at a certain point the formula switches direction and the more you put in the less you get out. In economics, this is known as the Law of Diminishing Returns.

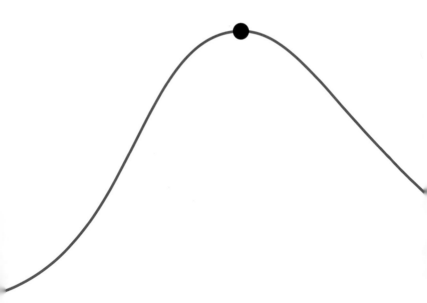

THE LAW OF DIMINISHING RETURNS

In all production processes, adding more of one factor of production, while holding all others constant, will at some point yield lower incremental per-unit returns.

Logic might suggest that if three painters can paint a house in five days, 15 painters should be able to paint a house in one! In reality, 15 painters end up getting in each other's way and not all are able to work at the same time in the same place, so it ends up taking longer and costing more.

Communication is no different. Our in-boxes would suggest that if three emails are good, 33 must be even better!

WE HAVE REACHED A POINT OF
PEAK COMMUNICATION, AND IT'S TIME
FOR A DRAMATIC CHANGE.

FOCUSED

COMMUNICATION

FOCUSED COMMUNICATION

In our first book, LESS & MORE, we introduced a new approach to help communication be more effective called: Focused Communication. This approach emphasizes action-oriented communication focused on achieving goals.

FOCUSED COMMUNICATION IS THE KEY
TO UNLOCKING THE POWER OF STREAMLINE.

5 PRINCIPLES OF
FOCUSED COMMUNICATION

IDEA ────────────────────────────────> OBJECTIVE

FOCUSED COMMUNICATION DIRECTLY CONNECTS AN IDEA TO AN OBJECTIVE.

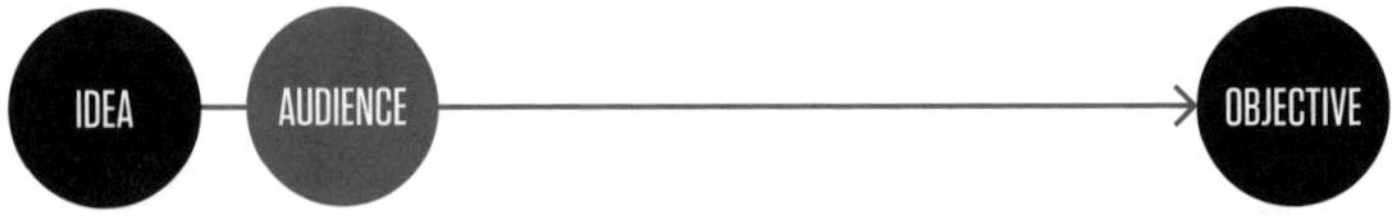
IDEA
AUDIENCE
OBJECTIVE

FOCUSED COMMUNICATION IS TAILORED SPECIFICALLY TO THE AUDIENCE.

FOCUSED COMMUNICATION STATES A STRAIGHTFORWARD MESSAGE.

4

FOCUSED COMMUNICATION USES APPROPRIATE TOOLS AND TECHNIQUES.

FOCUSED COMMUNICATION MAKES CLEAR THE ESSENTIAL ACTION.

IDEA — AUDIENCE — MESSAGE — TECHNIQUE — ACTION → OBJECTIVE

I A M T A → O

I AM TAO

TAO IS THE WAY.

TAO

Pronounced 'dow', TAO is a classic Chinese concept dating from the 6th century B.C.

Originally presented by philosopher Laozi in his work *Tao te Ching*, TAO has a number of ascribed meanings, all of which relate to "the way".

I AM TAO IS THE WAY OF
FOCUSED COMMUNICATION.

As a mnemonic, I AM TAO is a helpful way to remember the elements of Focused Communication.

I	IDEA
A	AUDIENCE
M	MESSAGE
T	TECHNIQUE
A	ACTION
O	OBJECTIVE

The phrase itself is a reminder of the core techniques for achieving Focused Communication, and one we will refer back throughout this book.

I AM TAO: IN PRACTICE

Dear Reader,

Modern communication has the potential to invigorate
organizations with an attitude focused on progress.

When we change from a defensive stance to an of-
fensive one, our communication stops slowing down
progress and quickly helps move ideas forward.

THIS BOOK IS FOR LEADERS
Making communication more effective is an incredible
opportunity for teams and organizations. Simple changes in how we communicate can pay amazing dividends
in efficiency and productivity.

THE BIG IDEAS
1. Less said means more done.
2. Focused communication makes ideas truly effective.
3. Effective ideas will change the world.

WHERE DO YOU START
Share the ideas in this book with your colleagues
and commit to practicing the principles of Focused
Communication everyday.

Viva la clarity!

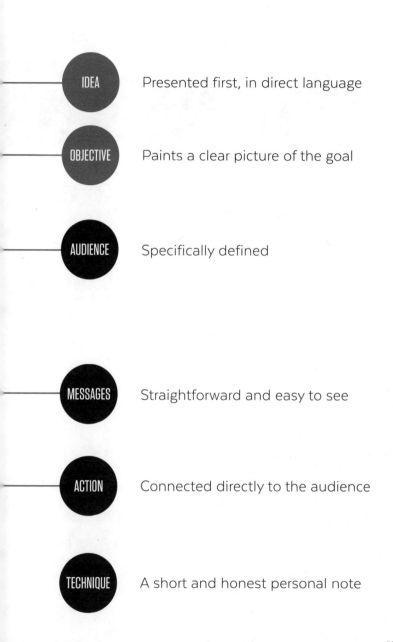

IDEA — Presented first, in direct language

OBJECTIVE — Paints a clear picture of the goal

AUDIENCE — Specifically defined

MESSAGES — Straightforward and easy to see

ACTION — Connected directly to the audience

TECHNIQUE — A short and honest personal note

INTRO TO STREAMLINING 101

You're likely familiar with the concept of streamlining when it comes to making planes, trains and auto-mobiles aerodynamic. A streamlined form for these vehicles minimizes their resistance as they move, and it allows them to move more easily at high speed, using less energy.

You may also have heard streamlining used in de-scribing processes, where the aim is to increase ef-ficiency by using simpler methods and fewer steps. For example, you might streamline an ordering process or checkout system.

In both cases, the intent is to address two factors that slow things down: FRICTION and DRAG.

FRICTON

Resistance from an outside source while in motion.

DRAG

A force that slows progress while in motion.

Communication can suffer from both of these factors.

WHAT IS STREAMLINING

The aim in streamlining communication is to shape our messages in ways that reduce friction and drag, allowing our ideas to move smoothly and efficiently towards their goal.

Streamlined communication removes the unnecessary complications in communication that cause messages to be misunderstood or misinterpreted. For example, in sending direct messages aimed at just the right individuals, the friction produced by complex, group-oriented communication can be eliminated.

Streamlining also focuses on the goal of good communication: Helping move ideas along with momentum. When we effectively streamline communication, we are able to stay focused on progress and not process.

STREAMLINED COMMUNICATION
IS AN EFFECTIVE MEANS TO AN END.

SWITCHING TO

OFFENSE

THE STORY OF MICHAEL

It was a typical Tuesday for Michael when he arrived at his desk early — excited to outline the things he needs to get done today. There are only four important items he must complete, and a fairly open day on his calendar, so he digs right in.

Michael has a few emails to respond to from the day before. A few of these were unclear so he shoots off some questions, completes what he can and empties his in-box before 9 AM. This is going to be a smooth day!

Turning his attention to the first item on his list, Michael is just getting his head around a complicated arrangement with a partner company when he receives a text from his boss — can he join her in a meeting at 3 PM this afternoon? He is happy for the invite and is quick to oblige.

As he turns back to his task, some replies to his earlier email questions start to arrive. One of his colleagues, Blair, is asking for a quick call to clear up a few items with the group instead of trying to answer by email. The call will be in 1/2 hour, not leaving Michael with enough time to finish his first project, so he shuffles his plans a bit to accommodate the call.

To kill some time ahead of the call, Michael pops onto the in-house chat platform to see what is going on. There is a spirited discussion happening about the kitchen on his floor and Michael lobs a playful suggestion about color-coded labels into the chat stream.

Turning to the team call, Michael makes small talk with his colleagues who joined on time, and they all wait for Blair. After ten minutes, the group receives an apologetic email from Blair who is stuck on another call. He needs to reschedule for 2 PM this afternoon.

It's 10:15 AM and Michael finally can dig into his first project.

Around 11 AM, Michael gets a text from his boss letting him know the 3 PM call has been moved to a lunch meeting — downtown. She knows this will be inconvenient for him, but if he can make it she will really appreciate it. Michael lets her know he'll be there and heads for the door. With traffic, he will just barely make the lunch meeting.

On the way out, Michael sends a text to his wife letting her know he won't be home for lunch as he'd planned. Two minutes later, Michael's wife calls and reminds him they needed to exchange cars at lunch so she could pick up the new dresser with his SUV. They negotiate and reshuffle their schedules with Michael planning to be at home by 4:30 PM so she can take his car.

During lunch, Michael can sense the work piling up as his phone buzzes with emails and group texts. He does his best to contribute to the lunch meeting, but the anxiety of his open tasks distract him. His boss notices.

Back from lunch, he remembers the 2 PM call was coming up and tries to complete his first task from the morning. He nearly wraps up, but some chatter on the instant message platform about his sassy food labeling idea draws him into a meaningless discussion about the cost of labeling machines.

Michael calls into the 2 PM team call that had been moved from this morning — where everyone finally joins after ten minutes of small talk. It turns out they needed to all look at a draft presentation - so they all switch to a WebEx call and are up and sharing by about 2:20 PM. A few people have to drop off at 2:30 PM and they ask for Michael to share any decisions that come from the call. Michael takes notes, watches the IM threads, and texts with his wife during the call just to try and keep up.

After the call, Michael sends out the notes and decisions made by the team, and by 3:30 PM he is able to refocus on his task list.

Emails keep arriving. Ding. Ding. The notes he sent out generate a slew of new questions and one of his team members needs the PowerPoint sent to him as a PDF since he is traveling and only has access through his phone. Twenty minutes later and Michael has wrapped up the "spontaneous meeting" from the morning!

Michael is watching the clock since he needs to be home by 4:30 PM — just as his boss calls to get his take on the lunch meeting. Michael tries to give her his full attention, but the texts, emails, IMs and his calendar all have reminders and notifications going off. The call does not go well.

He decides he is better off taking his computer home to work at night, so he packs up his bag and heads to the elevator — trying to slip out unnoticed. When the elevator arrives, he steps in, only to be greeted by the company President, Mr. Enso. The President quickly accesses the situation and quips, "Done for the day, Michael?"

"Not even close! Just going to work from home tonight, there are too many distractions here." Michael replies.

"Too many distractions, or not enough focus?" Mr. Enso rhetorically asks as the doors open and Michael steps into the parking garage. Mr. Enso does not leave the elevator.

Michael walks quickly to his car, only to realize his keys are in his jacket. Upstairs.

TOO MANY DISTRACTIONS,
OR NOT ENOUGH FOCUS?

FROM DEFENSE TO OFFENSE

THE MORAL OF THE STORY

What we see in the preceding story of Michael and in so many of our own habits, is that the balance of work and communication has become unreasonable.

Where once we used communication to augment our work, it is no longer uncommon for communication to trump our focus on work completely.

COMMUNICATION ABOUT WORK HAS BECOME
MORE IMPORTANT THAN THE WORK ITSELF.

The ever-growing collection of communication
channels funneling into our consciousness; emails,
texts, phone calls, instant messages, meetings, and
conference calls has shifted our attitude to a reac-
tionary (defensive) default. As a result, our effective
time to work has been sliced and diced into gaps
between communications.

COMMUNICATION HAS THE BIGGEST INFLUENCE
ON OUR PRODUCTIVITY.

Streamlined communication is designed to increase
both efficiency and effectiveness. When we adopt
the principles of streamlining, our communication
quickly allows us to spend more time playing
offense instead of defense.

To better understand and apply the Streamline approach to your own work, the next section offers a
two-step guide for Best Practices.

WORK

COMMUNICATION

VS

COMMUNICATION

WORK

BEST

PRACTICES

BEST PRACTICES
STEP 1: COMMUNICATION GUIDELINES

COMMUNICATION IS A TEAM SPORT.

The first step to playing an effective game is understanding the rules. Most organizations (teams) never take the time to come together and agree on the rules. Instead, everyone runs around with their own idea of what the rules are without sharing their perspective or inquiring about the perspective of others.

The first step for streamlining communication is agreeing on the rules.

What are the expected windows for team members to be available online during the week?

What about the weekend or on holidays?

What is the most effective way to reach a team member who is out of the office on a business trip? Text message? Email? Phone call? Skype? Slack?

These are just a few of the types of undefined scenarios for which we could likely find dozens of different and conflicting answers from team member to team member.

PRODUCTIVE GUIDELINES

For teams and organizations, the creation of communication guidelines can be an eye-opening process. Whether you have a small team of three co-founders building a startup or a group of hundreds working together around the globe, the simple act of agreeing on basic communication guidelines can pay immediate dividends.

A simple set of guidelines will allow everyone to quite literally "be on the same page" when it comes to expectations.

It's important everyone knows the rules you are establishing are guidelines, not hard policy; there are always exceptions to the rules. Everyone should be trusted to use their own best judgement in special situations and not be restricted by an overly rigid policy.

COMMUNICATION GUIDELINES

February 17, 2016

Streamline Baseline
StreamlineToolkit.com/baseline

Communication Channels

PRIMARY CHANNEL
EMAIL
This channel is our primary means of communication.
Use this as your default method of communicating within the company.

SECONDARY CHANNEL
TEXT
This channel is for use in situations where a quick response is needed.
Limit use of this channel to limit interrupting others.

HOTLINE
TELEPHONE
Use this channel only in occasions where it is critical to reach someone.
Use this channel only if the secondary channel is ineffective.
Limit use of this channel to limit interrupting others.

Expected Availability

WORKDAYS
9am - 6pm
SATURDAYS
10am - Noon
SUNDAYS
None
HOLIDAYS
None

These times represent windows for common availability.
Special circumstances may require access beyond these hours.
All times are relative to local time zone of individuals.

Email Etiquette

REPLY ALL
Avoid use, always select recipients
CC
Only involved parties
BCC
None
RECEIPT CONFIRMATION
Receipt is presumed, no reply needed

Keep emails short and to the point.
Insure that your subject line matches the subject of your email.
Be clear with any actions needed by stating these clearly.
Include deadlines with any requests.

PAGE 1 OF 2

©2016 Streamline Certified | StreamlineToolkit.com

February 17, 2016

n possible.

organization.

only.

Files

STORAGE PLATFORM
Dropbox
FILE NAMING
PROJECT NAME - Document Name v1

Do not include date in file names.
Use full number versioning without decimals (v1 > v2 > v3)

PAGE 2 OF 2

©2016 Streamline Certified | StreamlineToolkit.com

See the STREAMLINE GUIDELINES at:
StreamlineCertified.com/guidelines

61

EFFECTIVE GUIDELINES

DEFINE

The creation of the communication guidelines can be a collaborative process to ensure that multiple perspectives are being taken into account. By working on these with team members, the resulting decisions are far more likely to be respected and practiced as everyone has had a hand in their creation. The guideline outline that follows can give you a good starting point for the decisions to be discussed and made.

SHARE

Once you have created the guidelines, it is important that they be distributed across the team or organization to be certain everyone involved in regular communication is aware. Also, adding these guidelines to any on-boarding process or new-hire introduction can create a strong impact by reducing the typical learning curve for communication within an organization.

PRACTICE

As a team exercise, it is important that the guidelines be respected and followed with consistency. The spirit of the exercise is to help everyone become more efficient and remove confusion. We've found it's best for *enforcement* to take the form of *reinforcement* of these values. As the team collaborates in practicing these newly defined guidelines, the aim is for streamlined behavior to become second nature; a natural asset to the organization's culture.

THE STREAMLINE TOOLKIT

To help you create your own guidelines, we've created a free online toolkit. Visit the website below and create your own guidelines in just a few minutes. This can also make for a spirited team exercise at your next meeting!

StreamlineToolkit.com

SUGGESTED GUIDELINE TOPICS

COMMUNICATION CHANNELS

What are the primary, secondary, and emergency communication channels for your team?

What are reasonable expectations for response times across these channels?

EXPECTED AVAILABILITY

What is the expected availability for your team on work days, weekends and holidays?

EMAIL ETIQUETTE

Who is expected to be included in communication threads?

How does your team handle email chains and long threads?

VIRTUAL MEETINGS

What is the preferred tool for hosting virtual calls/meetings?

How are meeting and call invitations expected to be shared?

COLLABORATION

What tools or platform are preferred for collaborating on documents?

How are work-in-process comments and editing cycles managed across your team?

DOCUMENTS

What are the preferred formats for presentations, spreadsheets and written documents?

How are final documents shared and distributed inside and outside the team?

FILES

Where are shared files stored for the team?

What is the naming and versioning protocol for document files?

CASE STUDY:
SMCOV COMMUNICATION GUIDELINES

SMCOV operates a nimble team across offices in different time zones throughout the U.S. The team relies on email to keep everyone informed, and it was becoming clear that distributed team members were regularly working different hours with different preferred windows for communication.

At the same time, the leaders of SMCOV wanted to insure that their team was not working around the clock. The time needed to pause and step away from work is highly respected at SMCOV. Yet, with the wide ranging work windows, emails flowed throughout the company around the clock.

To address this, SMCOV took the remarkably simple — yet often overlooked — step of defining communication boundaries and expectations and sharing these with the entire team. These guidelines removed all ambiguity, replacing confusion with a sense of clarity knowing everyone was communicating with the same protocols.

SAMPLE SMCOV COMMUNICATION GUIDELINES

WINDOWS OF WORK

Weekdays	9am - COB local time
Weekends	None
Holidays	None

Communications outside of this window should not expect attention until the next work day window.

Be aware your local time and your recipient's time may differ and plan accordingly.

URGENT MESSAGES

For urgent messages outside of the work windows, please selectively use text messages to coordinate a call. Avoid conversational text messages when possible.

MEETING PREFERENCES

For meetings of more than two people, consider these preferences:

First Option:	Conference Call-In Line
Second Option:	Online virtual meeting
Third Option:	In-person meeting

OUTCOMES

After implementing a handful of meta-communication guidelines, SMCOV saw a number of improvements throughout the organization.

THOUGHTFUL PLANNING AHEAD
With the understanding of colleagues work windows, team members quickly adapted to this reality and planned communication accordingly. The simple fact of knowing that a colleague is not expected to give attention outside of their work window quickly caused most of the work and communication to adapt accordingly.

PRESSURE RELIEF
In knowing that everyone was working with the same expectations, the previous pressure to be available around the clock immediately reduced the pressure on team members.

COLLABORATION
The uniformity of the guidelines and respect at all levels in the organizations encouraged the spirit of working together instead of individually.

CONCLUSIONS

Meta-communication (communication about communication) is the cause of tremendous strain and anxiety within organizations. When there is little to no clarity, poor assumptions and false interpretations cause unnecessary confusion within the organization.

When we remove ambiguities and clearly define expectations, then communication can focus on the goals at hand and leave behind the inefficiency of second-guessing.

THE MORE WE COMMUNICATE ABOUT COMMUNICATION, THE LESS COMMUNICATION WE NEED.

BEST PRACTICES
STEP 2: MEMOS

Each of the following chapters conclude with a collection of friendly BEST PRACTICE MEMOS to be shared. These memos are designed to introduce and reinforce key streamline ideas in teachable moments.

COMMON SENSE IS THE FOUNDATION OF STREAMLINING, SO MANY OF THESE IDEAS MAY ALREADY BE FAMILIAR TO YOU.

These memos are available via StreamlineToolkit.com. From there you can share the Memos as links. You can also download the Memos to use as attachments or reminders when you encounter situations that could use some streamlining.

MEMOS PRESENT FRIENDLY REMINDERS OF CONCEPTS WE OFTEN KNOW BUT SOMETIMES OVERLOOK.

YOU GET
THE FEEDBACK
YOU ASK FOR.

The more clear you are on what you hope to receive for feedback, the more clear your feedback will be. Be specific about what you expect to get by asking with detail.

TWO

STREAMLINING

The following sections provide details and techniques for getting the most out of STREAMLINING in everyday work:

IN WRITING
MEETINGS & CALLS
DOCUMENTS
PRESENTATIONS
FEEDBACK

FUNDAMENTALS FOR

WRITING

It's 5:45pm and Catherine is one email away from in-box zero. It has taken her all day to get through them and she is sick of it. But freedom is near. She responds, copying everyone on her team - just in case.

It's Saturday and Kevin is cheering on his daughter at her soccer game when his phone buzzes. It's an email from his boss asking about the presentation for next week. He tries to turn back to the game but ends up texting another colleague to get a status update.

It's been 28 hours and Eric doesn't understand why no one has responded to his email. He spent so much time writing it – more than 2000 words of sheer brilliance!

We are overwhelmed by the written communication entering our lives.

But are we also part of the problem?

EXPECT MORE

CASE STUDY: BLUE SKY BANK

The email to the right is an example of a typical corporate email we've all encountered at one time or another. In this case, first contact is established between a representative of Blue Sky Bank and the president of a Home Owner's Association (HOA). The two have never spoken, never met, and have never had any contact.

This real-world example highlights the often over-looked opportunities available to us within every-day written communications. We have dissected this brief introduction in the pages ahead to shine a light on the friction and drag typically of non-streamlined messages.

SUBJECT: Questionnaire (Williamson)

Hello,

Can you please complete and return the attached questionnaire?

I also need the name or contact information for the Master Homeowners Insurance and/or copy of the Dec page.

Thank you,
Jessica Hargrave | Mortgage Sales Assistant
Residential Mortgage NMLS# 31211999
Blue Sky Bank | MC 1717
1717 Yorkville Avenue | Toronto, Ontario | M5R 1C2
P: 212-555-1212 | F:800-555-1213
JHargrave@BlueSkyBank.com

BLUE SKY BANK | expect more

Be aware that if you reply directly to this message, your reply may not be secure. Do not use e-mail to send us communications which contain unencrypted confidential information such as passwords, account numbers or Social Security numbers. If you must provide this type of information, please visit blueskybank.com to submit a secure form using any of the Contact Us forms. You should avoid sending any inquiry or request that may be time sensitive. The information in this e-mail is confidential – it is intended for the individual or entity to whom it is addressed. If you have received this e-mail in error, please destroy or delete the message and advise the sender of the error.

 Williamson Condo Quest bl.pdf

INITIAL READING

The previous email represents 'First Contact' between a bank representative and the president of an HOA, yet no context or introduction has been provided. When such vague messages are received, the reader is forced to decipher hidden meaning and ask themselves:

Is this junk mail?
Is this directed at me personally?
How important is this?
How much time will this take?
Is there a deadline?
What is the next action?

Let's take a closer look.

THE SUBJECT LINE

Questionnaire (Williamson)

The subject line gives very little explanation or context around the information contained within, which forces the reader to open the email and determine its relevance. If this email were received on a smart phone, you likely would scroll past not knowing or caring if this were spam. Had the subject line been better crafted, the reader could easily swipe to file the contents digitally (and mentally) and address it later.

REQUEST 1

Can you please complete and return the attached
questionnaire?

The real question is: Will you? Without any framing of this request, the reader is left to decipher the
purpose of the inquiry. More importantly, there is no
reference to a deadline; when does the sender need
this to be completed and returned? If a timeline
had been established, the urgency (or non-urgency)
would be obvious.

REQUEST 2

I also need the name or contact information for the Master
Homeowners Insurance and/or copy of the Dec page.

Although it is not clear, it seems the request is related to this Williamson's mortgage, but that is only
a guess. The sender has not been straightforward in
identifying her role, or the relationship with this Williamson client to the recipient of the email. This lack
of clarity makes it difficult to consider her request a
priority.

HER SIGNATURE

Thank you,

Jessica Hargrave | Mortgage Sales Assistant

Residential Mortgage NMLS# 31211999

Blue Sky Bank | MC 1717

1717 Yorkville Avenue | Toronto, Ontario | M5R 1C2

P: 212-555-1212 | F:800-555-1213

JHargrave@BlueSkyBank.com

Her signature is nearly longer than her communication! In fact, this is the first place we discover that this note is from a bank. It is not until the end of her message that we can finally see the source of her questions and can piece together the requests must be related to a financing change Mr. Williamson is making.

The pieces of the puzzle begin to take shape!

LEGAL DISCLAIMER

Here in the legal disclaimer included with her email.

Be aware that if you reply directly to this message, your reply may not be secure. Do not use e-mail to send us communications which contain unencrypted confidential information such as passwords, account numbers or Social Security numbers. If you must provide this type of information, please visit blueskybank.com to submit a secure form using any of the Contact Us forms. You should avoid sending any inquiry or request that may be time sensitive. The information in this e-mail is confidential – it is intended for the individual or entity to whom it is addressed. If you have received this e-mail in error, please destroy or delete the message and advise the sender of the error.

In reading this, we discover the ban does not consider email a safe or timely way to communicate, their website contains multiple "Contact Us" forms — and, it's very possible this email was not intended for you!

While many institutions require these appended legal disclaimers, they very often serve little purpose yet seem to create unnecessary clutter in communication chains.

ATTACHMENT

Williams Condo Quest bl.pdf

As we continue our sleuthing, we open the PDF to discover it is six pages long, contains 56 questions, and had been scanned from a paper document. The document has partial information filled in by hand. To complete this, it will mean printing it out, filling it out by hand, scanning, then returning.

BRANDING

BLUE SKY BANK | expect more

And finally, the logo of the company is included as a tiny graphic with their tag-line: EXPECT MORE.

Presumably, this bank wants us to raise our expectations of banking, by looking to them as the gold standard.

CHALLENGE ACCEPTED.

INVESTMENTS & RETURNS

From a fiscal perspective, here's a quick recap of the deal:

THE BANK
INVESTMENT THEY ARE WILLING TO MAKE
> 1 minute impersonal email
> 2-3 minutes of follow-up clarification emails
> Minimal effort and engagement

RETURN THEY EXPECT
> Opportunity to close a new mortgage
> Profit of a few thousand dollars

RECIPIENT (POTENTIAL CLIENT)
INVESTMENT ASKED OF THE RECEIVER
> Time spent parsing the email for context
> Time clarifying and replying to the requests
> 45-minutes completing paperwork

RETURN ON OUR INVESTMENT
> Negative engagement experience with the bank
> Disbelief in the bank's positioning: Expect More

STREAMLINING THE EMAIL

So, what could this exchange have looked like? With an investment of slightly more time, and an emphasis on helping the audience both understand and complete the tasks, it would be very easy to reverse the experience from negative to positive.

The revision at right illustrates the following:

IMPROVEMENTS
> Clear and functional subject line
> Proper context and introduction
> Clear tasks and actions to be taken
> Creation of an online form for easy completion
> Clear timing request
> Sincere empathy and appreciation
> Personal connection with a potential client

Ultimately, a small investment of time could transform an unfriendly and time-consuming exchange into a positive expression of the bank's message.

We should all EXPECT MORE from our bank and our communications!

SUBJECT: Condo details needed By July 25th
               for Mark Williams refinancing

Hello Raj,

Our bank is working with a neighbor of yours, Mark Williams, to refinance his mortgage. He gave me your name and email as the person responsible for the HOA.

To help us complete his paperwork, we will need two (2) things from you:

1. MASTER HOMEOWNERS INSURANCE
> Copy of the declarations page - or -
> Contact information for the insurance company

2. ONLINE QUESTIONNAIRE
The link below has a questionnaire you can complete online.
> bit.ly/BSBQuestionnaire

DUE DATE: JULY 25th
We aim to complete Mark's paperwork by August 1st, so if you can find the time to address these by our due date it would be a great help.

We know these requests can be time-consuming, and we truly appreciate you helping out your neighbor. As a thank you, I'd love to offer you access to our premium refinancing service in the future. Just contact me directly if you would like a free consultation.

Jessica Hargrave
Mortgage Assistant, Blue Sky Bank
212-555-1212 | JHargrave@BlueSkyBank.com
Expect more.

STREAMLINING WRITTEN COMMUNICATION

THE STATE OF THE ART

Written communication has undergone a dramatic evolution within the past 30 years. As technology evolved, so too have our methods of sharing and read- ing. Where the skill of typing was once a specialized area of focus for a select few, keyboard use has become the basis for everything; from writing computer code to texting our parents. The proliferation of the written word, has never been greater.

In particular, within business communications, we have seen a number of fundamental shifts take place that have revealed new dynamics for written communications worth reviewing.

TRENDS

The blurring of lines between personal and work communications have led to an influx of casual communication characteristics throughout traditionally formal business writing.

Social sharing and the integration of social platforms within business (for marketing and feedback for instance) have further blurred the etiquette and style expectations.

Expanding remote workforces have created virtual replacements for the office water-cooler, where team members can gather and chat from anywhere in the world.

These trends and others show no sign of slowing down, making it clear how important it is for teams and organizations to have strong guidelines and strategies for written communication.

CHANNELS

Modern written communication is organized into various channels, each with a particular style and approach. Like TV channels, we come to expect certain types of messages to come through each of these different channels.

While these may be our expectations, in truth, the lines between each of these channels are not clearly defined. It is this very lack of definition and blurring at the edges, which causes much of the confusion and distress we experience with modern communication.

AGREEMENT ON HOW TO USE DIFFERENT
CHANNELS IS THE FOUNDATION FOR AN
EFFECTIVE COMMUNICATION ENVIRONMENT.

A GROWING VARIETY OF CHANNELS

EMAIL
sequential messages across individuals & teams

INSTANT MESSAGES (Texts, iMessages, etc)
1-to-1 messages for immediate attention

CHAT (Skype, Slack, etc.)
many-to-many messages for conversations

DIGITAL DOCUMENTS
distribution of formalized ideas and results

SOCIAL PLATFORMS (Twitter, Facebook, etc.)
personal expression

TIMING: NOW VS. LATER

One clear way to approach these channels is to consider how each relates to the timing of communication. Almost all communication is an exchange back and forth between people, and the timing of that exchange is a big factor in how a channel should be used.

SYNCHRONOUS CHANNELS

For most of our history, the common type of communication was between people in the same place at the same time having a conversation. Two or more people discussing a topic in the same room creates a very dynamic exchange that can quickly change direction, reach resolution, or simply answer questions without delay.

We see this in today's work environment as meetings & conference calls. Where these discussions once required everyone to be in the same place, technology has made it possible to hold these synchronous exchanges by audio and video calls with people distributed around the world.

ASYNCHRONOUS CHANNELS

As people spread further apart, it was necessary to create new channels for discussion that allowed for exchanges that couldn't happen in real-time. The simple act of writing letters bridged tremendous gaps of space between individuals — while adding a gap of time as well. Knowing that your recipient cannot immediately reply quickly changes the nature of the communication significantly.

Asynchronous communication, which has evolved from letter-writing to email, creates an important buffer for thought in the communication exchange. Both the sender and receiver are afforded greater time for thoughtful consideration and organization of their ideas before sharing them — an important distinction in our fast-paced world.

CHANNELS: DECIDE & DEFINE

Understanding and consciously electing when to use which path is a critical aspect in designing an efficient communication strategy. When we select and agree to use one channel for synchronous communication and another channel for asynchronous communication, the ambiguity of expectations is eliminated.

EVERYONE SHOULD KNOW WHAT TO EXPECT
AND WHAT IS EXPECTED.

Marcus is the leader of a large team. Since he works for a well-known company he is a powerful client for many vendors. He is very organized and considers himself a productivity master. Marcus has a habit of sending emails with requests for follow-up late on Friday afternoons and throughout just about any holiday. He sees it as a great way to empty his mind so that he can fully enjoy his time with his family.

But has he considered what impact he is having on his recipients?

Communication is always a two-way street. While it may be convenient and freeing to send off messages to clear your mind, those same thoughts are now the focus of your audience.

When we practice the art of considering our audience, we quickly learn that it is often as important to understand when our message will be received as when it is sent.

Process and compose your messages when it is convenient for you, but send them (or delay delivery) for when they will be best for your audience to consider.

FOCUSED COMMUNICATION:

WRITTEN COMMUNICATION

A powerful way to streamline writing is to apply the Focused Communication principles to make clear the path from **IDEA** to **OBJECTIVE**.

Here we have the **I AM TAO** framework put to the test to see how this applies to writing.

With your **IDEA** and **OBJECTIVE** defined, you can then identify the **AUDIENCE**, **MESSAGE**, **TECHNIQUE**, and **ACTION** for making the connections.

AUDIENCE

FOCUS ON YOUR PRIMARY AUDIENCE
Limit your audience to only those who have a direct connection to the objective of your message. Every person you include in an email dilutes its impact and focus to the individuals you are addressing. When in doubt, don't cc: or bcc: anyone else.

ADDRESS YOUR AUDIENCE SPECIFICALLY
Address each individual to insure that the recipient quickly knows the message is intended for them. Sending messages to a "Team" or not addressing anyone by name misses an opportunity to connect your audience with your message.

ALWAYS CONSIDER THE CONTEXT FOR RECEIPT
Where will your audience be when they receive your message? You should always consciously consider the time, location and context when you expect your message will be read and adjust accordingly. A message to a traveling colleague can respect the difference in time-zone and high-potential for distraction. Your audience will appreciate your thoughtfulness.

MESSAGE

POWERFUL SUBJECT LINES

The subject line of an email can be extremely valuable for conveying the true nature of your message. Consider that within dense in-boxes (especially on mobile phones), the subject line is most likely the only thing your audience will see when they scan their incoming messages. The subject line can contain the answer to questions, important changes to schedules or plans, and in some cases may be the entire message itself.

SUBJECT:

re: Design Finals Needed - RECEIVED - Expect by noon

SUBJECT:

re: Meeting Friday> - CONFIRMED @3:00 via Skype

SUBJECT:

Thursday team call postponed to Monday @11am - EOM*

---

*EOM = End Of Message - indicates there is no need to look any further.

MESSAGE FIRST, CONTEXT SECOND

Military officials are trained to begin their communication by stating the bottom line of any communication first. Known as BLUF for Bottom Line Up Front, this method recognizes that time is most always of the essence, and the key message should not get lost in the middle or fall to the end.

When you practice the BLUF technique, you begin with the salient points or decisions so your message does not have to be parsed. Once you present your key points, you can then follow up with the relevant details and context. Too often we craft messages that work through our logic and thinking, building up to the conclusion. Reversing this approach is much more efficient and effective.

TECHNIQUE

HEADLINES FOR SCANNING

Breaking up your message into scannable sections, each with a descriptive headline, recognizes that most people do not always have the time to carefully read your full message. With headlined sections, the message contents are easily understood in a split second, allowing your audience to prioritize where they should focus.

CALL OUT REFERENCE INFORMATION

When you include information in your message which you know your audience will need to reference — like addresses, dates and times — you should make an effort to increase the accessibility of this information. Instead of including it within the sentences of your message, separate and indent it so that it can be easily spotted when needed.

REVIEW CALL - Design Team
Tuesday, April 26th
9:00am CST via Skype

ACTION

WHAT TO-DO

When you are asking someone to do something specific, present your request in a way that is easy for them to translate into their own to-do item. Like the reference information, actions can be separated and made explicitly clear to avoid any confusion.

> POSTCARD DESIGN FINALS - Approved > To printer today

> FLYER DESIGN - Match brand colors > for approval by EOD

I A M T

Recall, the ACTION is what ultimately gets us to the OBJECTIVE.

The next section highlights other best practices for streamlining writing across many other areas of communication.

STREAMLINING EMAIL SIGNATURES

KEEP IT SIMPLE.
HAVE TWO VERSIONS.

PRIMARY SIGNATURE

Your primary signature is used in daily exchanges with colleagues and contacts whom all already have your contact information. There is no need to include all of your ancillary information in these common exchanges; it only adds unnecessary information that is always skipped.

> Full Name

> Email address

> Direct phone number only

INTRODUCTION SIGNATURE

Create a separate signature, different from your shorter default signature, to use in special exchanges with new contacts. This more detailed signature provides a full picture of your role and ancillary contact information, but still avoids common elements that are distracting and ineffective — like marketing messages and inspirational quotes.

When your email program only allows for a single signature (like Gmail), aim to limit the number of lines that the signature consumes. Placing secondary information together on a single line helps streamline your signature.

> Full Name, Title

> Email address

> Direct phone number only

> Company Name | Company web address

EMAIL DISCLAIMERS

"LEGAL" DISCLAIMERS

In short, these disclaimers so often appended to emails have no legal value and are unenforceable in almost all situations. Despite their ubiquity, these "legal" messages offer virtually no protection and provide a false sense of security. No one reads them and they serve no real purpose beyond exponentially expanding every email thread where they are repeated over and over.

The best security is being careful when you compose and address your email, because once you hit send, there's no putting the genie back in the bottle!

EMAIL DEAD WEIGHT

This message is intended only for the use of the addressees shown above, but I must have hit 'send' too fast. It might contain information that may be privileged, confidential and/or exempt from disclosure under applicable law, but that really has no bearing here because I made the mistake of sending it to you. If you are not the intended recipient of this message, you are hereby notified that the review, copying, distribution or other use of any information or materials transmitted in or with this message is strictly prohibited – just a friendly tip that is not enforceable, FYI. If you have received this communication in error, please immediately notify us by return e-mail and promptly delete the original electronic e-mail communication and any attached documentation. We do realize that you won't do this and there's no real way to delete e-mails entirely, so, yeah I guess I should have thought twice before hitting send.

FRIENDLY FOOTERS

FEELING INSPIRED
Motivational quotes and inspirational messages in email signatures have a very short half-life. They may be read once, but every communication that follows simply gets burdened by these unread and unnecessary components.

Instead of a generic, unspecific inspiration, try connecting with your audience sincerely with personal thoughts that reinforce your message. Personal words will always provide more of an impact than a virtual bumper sticker.

PROMOTIONS
Much like the disclaimers and inspirations, promotions placed in email signatures come across as insincere. Furthermore, they significantly increase the chance that your message can be filtered out as spam!

Keep your signatures simple and personal or risk looking like a robot to the world.

STREAMLINING ATTACHMENTS

JUST SAY NO

Attachments are the potholes of the internet high-way. Whenever we attach a file to an email, we create a copy of that document and force our recipients to store and/or file it. Over time, these files (large and small) weigh down our email systems as they become filing cabinets filled with copies and copies of files that are difficult to find or organize. Avoid frivolous attachments and consider an alternative sharing method whenever possible.

STREAMLINING SHARED FILES

Cloud-based technologies make it easy to organize and store files in a central repository which can then be linked to instead of shared. Using this technique, we eliminate the duplication factor and encourage a collaborative organization where teams maintain shared files that don't get out of sync.

STREAMLINING CONFIRMATIONS

FULL STOP

Efficient communication focuses on reducing traffic by eliminating unnecessary communication loops. Recipients who feel the need to reply to an email with a short "Got it." or "Thanks!" are often reacting to an environment of uncertainty. Communication between professionals should give the benefit of the doubt to both the sender and the receiver. Your message should be assumed to have been received and understood.

Messages can also be smartly framed so that it is clear that a non-reply is a confirmation. This simple act of strategically closing communication loops can make huge strides towards a more empty in-box.

Unless I hear from you, I will plan to call you Wednesday at 2:00 your time. NNTR*

---

*NNTR = No Need To Reply

IN REVIEW: ALL EMAIL BEST PRACTICES

TO: Sharon Swift (sharon@zerogravity.com)

SUBJECT: HEXXIS LAUNCH EVENT - CONFIRMED ————————
                Fri. Nov 17 @ 3:00p - The Village, 969 Market St.

Sharon,

I'm happy to report we have selected our event space for the HEXXIS
launch event. We are confirmed at The Village (also known as 969
Market Street) for Friday, Nov. 17th, from 4:00pm to 10:00pm. Below
is a brief agenda for our meeting tomorrow morning:

MARKETING DISCUSSION ————————————————————————

> Final press release copy - for approval

> Final marketing collateral - for approval

> Special guest speaker – Dorothy Parker, CEO, She Got Game

> Investor dinner

> Timeline > deadlines

> Marketing budget recap

PLEASE REVIEW ————————————————————————————————

I'd like for you to take a look at the website for the venue of the event.
I think you will be as excited as I am.

        LAUNCH EVENT VENUE ————————————————————
        Website: http://969market.com

: : : : :

Leah Sky ————————————————————————————————
Leah@ZeroGravityGames.com
1-212-555-1212

FUNCTIONAL SUBJECT LINE

HEADLINING TOPICS

DEFINED ACTION

REFERENCE INFORMATION CALLED OUT

SIMPLE SIGNATURE

EVERYTHING YOU REMOVE
MAKES EVERYTHING THAT REMAINS
MORE CLEAR.

STREAMLINING PAYS OFF

Streamlining our written communication has one of the most measurable returns on investment. With the aim of reducing or eliminating unnecessary communications and communication loops, streamlining is a powerful offense in a landscape accustomed to playing defense.

INVEST TIME TO SAVE TIME

Creating thoughtful messages that are clear, focused and easy on which to act requires some practice and commitment at first. However, over time, the more straight-forward approach will become a style that comes naturally and quickly.

EDIT FOR IMPACT

Reread every message before you send it and consider what unnecessary pieces can be removed to make your central message make more of an impact. Remember that everything you remove makes everything that remains more clear.

PRIORITIZE ACTION

Focus your message around the action that needs to be taken to move closer to your mutual objective. Your audience is often looking for direction and definition on what to do next. When we make the action the priority, our communication becomes streamlined with ease.

YOUR SUBJECT LINE MUST MATCH YOUR SUBJECT.

Your subject line is like the cover of your book — it impacts whether someone will want to open and read it. Make it relevant. Make it helpful.

REREAD EVERY MESSAGE BEFORE YOUR SEND IT.

Catch mistakes, correct and simplify your language, and delete unnecessary information when you reread your message before sending it.

AVOID ASKING OTHERS TO 'SEE BELOW'.

Always summarize the context and content to which you're referring instead of forcing your audience to play detective and uncover the importance of a message.

ALWAYS BREAK A THREADED CONVERSATION WHEN THE TOPIC CHANGES.

Change the subject line and do not include the thread history when the topic changes. New ideas deserve new messages.

FUNDAMENTALS FOR

MEETINGS &
CALLS

"Any questions?"
The conference room went silent. Why bring up
any real concerns? The decision had already been
made long before the meeting began.

Sophia looked up at the clock — nearly the end of
the hour. Almost there. It had been ten minutes
and two of her colleagues were still debating over a
matter that had nothing to do with her.

Peter had never felt so proud - a new Angry Birds
high score! The conference call continued to drone
on in the background.

Have you ever been in a meeting like this?

Have you ever run a meeting like this?

STREAMLINING MEETINGS & CALLS

SEE WHAT I'M SAYING?

The instinct for people to get together and discuss ideas is natural. In-person communication is incredibly rich with characteristics so often lost in writing.

NON-VERBAL COMMUNICATION

Body language	Tone and speed of delivery
Eye contact	Facial reactions

Meetings and calls are also by their nature synchronous, creating an environment where dynamic discussion and engagement is the norm. The extremely high-value of live, in-person engagements is without doubt.

However, in the modern business world, when you ask individuals what parts of their day are most productive, most efficient or most enjoyable, meetings and calls hover at the bottom of almost everyone's list.

When we look at meetings & calls through the lens of Focused Communication, there are tremendous opportunities to streamline for more efficient and effective communications.

FOUR TYPES OF MEETINGS

There are basically four types of meetings that are popular in today's business culture.

IN PERSON-MEETINGS

Meetings where everyone is together in the same physical space and can readily interact and talk with each other. These are the benchmark for high quality, engaging discussions that make meetings valuable. A conference meeting, team meeting, or even spontaneous meeting of two individuals in the hallway each share the many benefits of in-person interactions.

VIDEO MEETINGS

Video technology has evolved to approximate the experience of the in-person meeting, yet still allows individuals to be distributed across multiple locations. While these meetings do allow us to see each other and engage in ways similar to how we do in person, they still suffer from limitations — like the lack of direct eye-contact and the inability to have sideline discussions like we can in-person. Unfortunately, the technology involved means it's not always easy to arrange or attend these video connections.

AUGMENTED CALLS

Another popular format for meetings has evolved from our presentation-oriented business culture. Sharing slides or documents for discussion on a call has become a norm via screen-sharing software. These augmented conference calls allow a group to easily be on the same page at the same time while still working from different locations. On the downside, the lack of non-verbal interaction can quickly reduce clarity in these meetings.

CONFERENCE CALLS

Conference calls provide a convenient method for gathering individuals across multiple locations. The interactions are fairly limiting, as much about our colleagues actions and reactions are left to the imagination. How do we interpret silence on the line? Do we know if everyone is really paying attention, or are they focused on something else? Ultimately, conference calls favor convenience over quality in most instances.

UNDERSTANDING MEETING FORMATS

For each of these meeting types there are benefits to gain and trade-offs to be made. When we understand that each of the formats has unique values, we can weigh the factors that are important to us and select accordingly. Understanding these strengths and weaknesses of each format can also be valuable as we participate. When we accept that not all meetings are created equal, we can begin to adapt our use and expectations.

ENGAGEMENT
How well will the contributors be able to share, listen and interact?

CONVENIENCE
How easy is it for each individual to participate from where they work?

EFFICIENCY
How easy is it for participants to attend with little notice given?

EFFECTIVENESS
What is the likelihood of having a meaningful exchange and outcome?

A comparison of meeting types across key factors. Consider the strengths and weaknesses of each when selecting the appropriate engagement for the goals you have.

	IN-PERSON MEETINGS	VIDEO MEETINGS	AUGMENTED CALLS	CONFERENCE CALLS
ENGAGEMENT	● (large)	● (medium)	● (small)	● (small)
CONVENIENCE	● (small)	● (small)	● (large)	● (large)
EFFICIENCY	● (medium)	● (large)	● (large)	● (large)
EFFECTIVENESS	● (large)	● (large)	● (medium)	● (medium)

FOCUSED COMMUNICATION:
MEETINGS & CALLS

Applying the I AM TAO framework allows us to provide a streamlined approach to meetings & calls. While many of these concepts are common sense or Business 101, they are worth revisiting if only to highlight how Focused Communication applies to all forms of business communication.

IDEA

WHAT IS THE PURPOSE OF THE MEETING
Every meeting is initiated because of an idea. The catalyst for a valuable meeting typically focuses on a need, such as:

A discussion on a specific matter

Gathering feedback and opinions

Looking for insight

Making a decision

AUDIENCE

WHO HAS AN INTEGRAL ROLE
IN REACHING THE OBJECTIVE

Limit the audience for a meeting to only those who have a true role in moving toward the objective. Everyone in a meeting is expected to contribute.

Everyone in a meeting should be a participant, not an attendee.

BE RESPECTFUL OF THE COMMITMENT
YOU ARE ASKING OF OTHERS

Attending a meeting means committing time to prepare, attend and focus on one thing at the expense of not focusing somewhere else. We all know the value of our own time, and we must respect the time of others equally.

When in doubt, don't invite.

MESSAGE

KEEP THE SCOPE OF THE MEETING FOCUSED
It's quite easy to get off track in discussions when a group of people are encouraged to engage and share. A leader focused on the objective can find a balance that embraces sharing and reigns in tangents.

It is the role of the leader to steer the conversation.

TECHNIQUE

USE THE TIME TOGETHER FOR DISCUSSION, NOT SHARING
The highest value from gathering people together is from facilitating interaction. A group of people assembled to receive information or watch a presentation is not a meeting. Prepare the participants ahead of a meeting by sharing what you expect everyone to know so that the time together is spent in discussion, not silence.

Share materials ahead of a meeting, not during.

ACTION

EFFECTIVE MEETINGS REACH A CONCLUSION
OR MAKE A DECISION

The purpose of most meetings is to move forward
by collective consent. The nature of discussions can
sometimes make it unclear whether progress has
been made. Ensure that your meeting concludes
clearly with everyone who has participated knowing
exactly what has been resolved.

A meeting is over when the decisions have been made.

OBJECTIVE

WHAT IS EXPECTED AS A RESULT OF
THE MEETING

Meetings can be important steps in moving ideas or
projects forward. An effective meeting has a clearly
defined objective that is the focus. This objective
is best presented before or at the very beginning of
the meeting.

Make sure everyone knows the destination
before they jump in the car.

LET'S HAVE A MEETING

A very effective way to streamline meetings & calls is to consider whether one is needed or not. The thinking that leads us to call for a meeting can be fine-tuned when we consider the value and expectations we have from gathering a group together.

The list below is a good reference for needs a meeting or call can fulfill.

- ☑ Focused discussions
- ☑ Active feedback
- ☑ Opportunity for explaining
- ☑ Opportunity for listening
- ☑ Chance to question
- ☑ Soliciting opinions & perspectives
- ☑ Collective decision-making

LET'S NOT

Oftentimes we confuse the act of gathering people together with a meeting. There are a multitude of group interactions that do not require a meeting of everyone in the same place at the same time. When we recognize these situations, we can easily take a different path.

- ✖ Simply sharing information
- ✖ Telling without a need for reaction or feedback
- ✖ Distributing materials
- ✖ Reviewing something collectively

All of these are examples where it may be convenient to the organizer to gather a group together, but it is not efficient for the audience. As workplaces becoming decentralized and distributed, it's critical that the good of the group transcends the need of an individual when it comes to structured meet-ups. Choose another asynchronous option for these needs whenever possible.

A valuable meeting is one where
everyone attending wants to participate.

STREAMLINING IN PRACTICE:
IN-PERSON MEETINGS

MAKE MEETINGS THE OPTION OF LAST RESORT
For most people, the best meetings are the ones
that never happen. Respect the schedules and
commitments of your colleagues by striving to
move forward with an asynchronous path. Only call
for meetings when it is absolutely necessary. Your
team will thank you.

PARTICIPANTS NOT ATTENDEES
Invite only those who have an active stake in the
meeting topic and who you expect will contribute
to the discussion. Anyone who does not meet these
criteria can receive a summary after the meeting.

SHARE AHEAD
Avoid using the collective time of everyone in a meeting to simply share information.

Provide as much material and information ahead of a meeting, and expect everyone to come to the meeting prepared to discuss and share their perspectives.

KNOW WHEN TO END A MEETING
Meetings get scheduled for windows of time and end up taking up that time by default. Be prepared to end a meeting when the discussion and decisions are made — not just because the next meeting is starting.

STREAMLINING VIDEO MEETINGS

STAY FOCUSED

With the convenience of attending a meeting from your computer, it is tempting to split your attention with other distractions. Treat a video meeting exactly as you would an in-person meeting by giving your full focus and attention. When you don't, everyone else can easily tell — you're not fooling anyone.

LIGHTING 101

Make an effort to insure that your face is well lit. By turning off lighting behind you and having lights in front of you, your face will be much clearer and you can make a better connection with your colleagues. There's no point in being in a video meeting if you can't be seen clearly.

MAKE A CONNECTION

Enlarge the video of your colleagues as large as possible on your screen (full screen if possible) so that you can best emulate being together with them. Sit close to the camera so your face fills in at least 30% of the screen. When you sit back and appear small, others won't be able to connect with your facial expressions. Lastly, make an effort to look at the camera itself when you speak — this allows others to make eye contact with you while you talk.

STREAMLINING AUGMENTED CALLS

MASTER THE TECHNOLOGY

Screen-sharing software continually improves, leading to regular software updates and changing features. Invest the few minutes it takes to familiarize yourself with the latest features so that you can get the most from these calls. As a rule of thumb, always begin the process of hosting or joining a video call at least 5-minutes ahead of the scheduled start time to allow for last minute technology glitches.

SMILE, YOU'RE ON CAMERA

Most screen-sharing platforms include an option to share your webcam video along with your screen. When you include this small video of yourself along with your content, you have an opportunity to truly make a connection with your colleagues through what you are sharing: your screen + voice + video make for a powerful virtual meeting.

DON'T OVERSHARE

Be aware that sharing your screen can often mean sharing everything on your desktop. Consider what others can see and take precautions to close or hide anything that could be distracting:

BE AWARE OF PERSONAL INFORMATION IN:

Desktop wallpapers

Incoming emails

Calendar notifications

To-do lists

Open web browser tabs

Files on your desktop

STREAMLINING CONFERENCE CALLS

MASTER MUTE

Modern phones have highly sensitive microphones which pickup even the faintest of noises. Simply shuffling papers can sound like a tornado — let alone the barking dog outside that sounds like its on your lap. Master the art of muting yourself when you are not speaking to keep as clear a line as possible for everyone else.

SPEAKERPHONE ETIQUETTE

Make a habit of announcing your name before you speak ("This is Sabrina in Madrid...") as a courtesy to those on the call who may not know your voice. Also be conscientious of where the microphones are in the room and stay as close to them as possible. Larger rooms with multiple people quickly become difficult for off-site colleagues to parse individual voices that are further away from the microphones.

THE FEWER PEOPLE IN A MEETING, THE MORE GETS ACCOMPLISHED.

Less is more.

WHEN YOU'RE CONNECTING ON CAMERA, BEHAVE AS YOU WOULD IN PERSON.

Look your audience in the eye and speak directly to them. Give your full attention or stay off camera.

USE THE LOWEST COMMON DENOMINATOR FOR MEETING TECHNOLOGY.

Only require technology in which all team members are proficient. New platforms have a way of complicating and not simplifying the connections.

ALWAYS SEND AHEAD ANYTHING THAT WILL BE SHARED IN A MEETING.

Allow attendees to review and digest information. Expect participants to come prepared to discuss and ask questions rather than you spend the meeting sharing.

FUNDAMENTALS FOR

DOCUMENTS

What did she say again? Two days into his new role and Daniel was struggling to keep track of it all. He had already interrupted his boss three times that morning — if only the process was documented...

Emma was horrified. She had sent the wrong proposal to a top new prospect. She had accidentally attached a proposal created for a different client. How had this happened?

Marco's head was starting to hurt — the maze of figures in this spreadsheet wasn't making any sense. What were they trying to communicate?

Are documents an effective part of your toolbox or are they slowing you down?

STREAMLINING DOCUMENTS

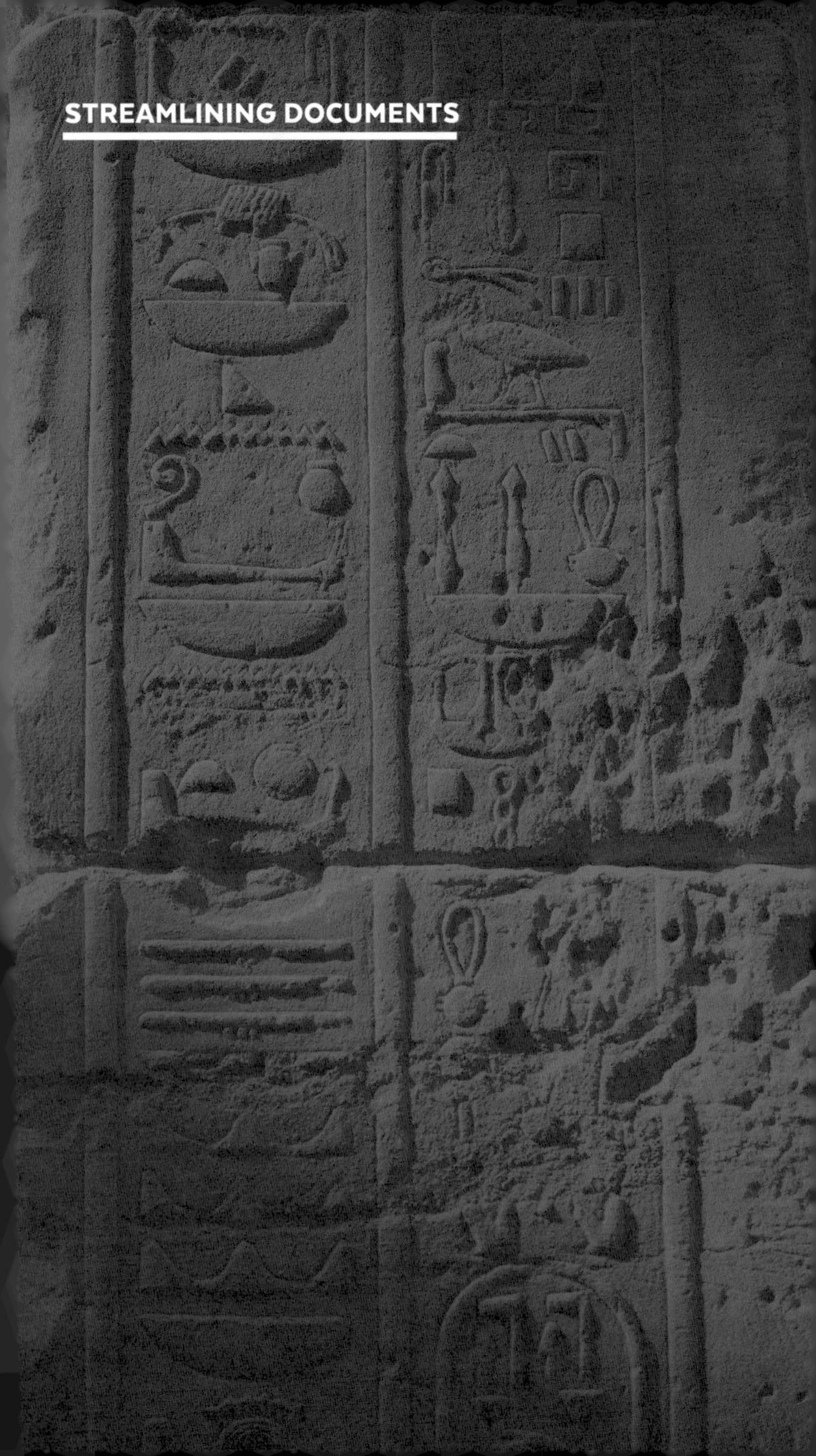

SET IN STONE

Where meetings and calls are the mortar of business communication, documents are the bricks. Documents allow us to take the ideas, discussions and decisions of everyday interactions and preserve them in a format that is designed to last. Documents are the foundation for business communication.

DOCUMENT

noun

A piece of written, printed, or electronic matter that provides information or that serves as an official record.

verb

To record something in written, photographic or other long-lasting form.

Documents give us the ability to freeze and capture information at a particular moment in time. Without them, communication would be full of ambiguity — not clarity.

DOCUMENTS ARE THE RECORDS OF IDEAS, INFORMATION AND DECISIONS THAT ALLOW BUSINESS TO GET DONE.

MESSAGES VS. DOCUMENTS

The line between these two very different pieces of communication has become blurred in our digital culture. We see messages (like emails) utilized to capture information for future use, and documents created when a conversation would be far more effective. For example, when providing feedback on a project.

Recognizing and understanding the difference between messages and documents goes a long way toward using each appropriately.

MESSAGES

DYNAMIC

Messages are designed for engagement

FOCUSED AUDIENCE

Messages are targeted at a focused audience

ONE-TIME USE

Messages are transitory and designed
for momentary use

DOCUMENTS

STATIC

Documents are designed to freeze
information at a moment in time

BROAD AUDIENCE

Documents are designed for a broad, and
oftentimes, undefined audience

REUSE

Documents are designed for use
multiple times in multiple situations

SYMBIOSIS

The relationship between messages and documents is symbiotic — they both rely on and benefit from the other. Documents almost always are accompanied by a message that explains the context and highlights their value. Once introduced, the documents can stand on their own. Consider some common examples:

DOCUMENT	+	MESSAGE
Resume	+	Cover letter
Attached File	+	Email
Report	+	Meeting discussion

All of these documents are made stronger with the framing provided by the accompanying message. Streamlining embraces the strengths of each communication component and practices using them together.

WHEN MESSAGES AND DOCUMENTS ARE
USED TOGETHER SMARTLY, COMMUNICATION
BECOMES MORE EFFICIENT AND EFFECTIVE.

UNDERSTANDING COMMON DOCUMENT TYPES

WRITTEN DOCUMENTS

The most common type of information.

Excellent for conveying depth & detail.

Tools like Word, Pages and Google Docs.

A basic skill level is needed to create effective documents.

DATA DOCUMENTS

Numbers and figures — very valuable modern information.

Powerful for organizing and analyzing.

Tools like Excel, Numbers and Google Sheets.

Specialized skills are required to create valuable documents.

VISUAL DOCUMENTS

Charts, graphs, illustrations and photos.

Effective for conveying concepts and conclusions.

Tools like stock photography, charting software.

Requires a trained eye to craft strong documents.

STORYTELLING DOCUMENTS

Mixing words + data + visuals in a single document.

An important tool for delivering messages that have impact.

Tools like PowerPoint, Keynote and InDesign.

Requires a talent to craft powerful documents.

IF ALL YOU HAVE IS A HAMMER,
EVERY PROBLEM LOOKS LIKE A NAIL.

IN THE REAL WORLD

OUR FAVORITE HAMMER

Despite the rich opportunity to know how to use a variety of tools for communication, many of us tend to rely on only one or two tools to create all of our documents. By using our favorite "hammer" every day, we may become proficient with it, but we are missing opportunities to use more appropriate solutions.

A DEEPER TOOLKIT

When we invest the time to become proficient with more tools, the return on that investment can be exponential. Each tool has a way of magnifying our skills and creating efficiencies that translate into stronger and richer communication.

CREATING DOCUMENTS THAT MAKE AN IMPACT IS KEY TO GIVING OUR IDEAS MOMENTUM.

FOCUSED COMMUNICATION:
STREAMLINING DOCUMENTS

We can apply the principles of Focused Communication to every document we create. Once we have defined our IDEA, a clear path can be created to meet our OBJECTIVE.

AUDIENCE

THE RIGHT DOCUMENT FOR THE AUDIENCE

The aim of our communication is to make an impact on our audience. When we look at this objective through their eyes, we will sometimes see that the right document for them is different from the document we may want to create. For instance, an audience focused on the numbers needs a different document than a highly visual audience. The audience and objective determine the proper tool.

MESSAGE

MAKE THE MESSAGE OBVIOUS
Many documents become dense with information and commentary, leaving the message lost in the mix. When you make the message the center of your document — presented clearly and upfront — everything else you include has a clear role to play in supporting your message.

TECHNIQUE

LEVERAGE DOCUMENT STRENGTHS
Each document type has its inherent strengths and weaknesses. Data documents are excellent tools for conveying facts and comparisons while written documents can better present depth and details. Along with considering the audience, selecting the right document format can streamline the message you aim to convey.

The **ACTION** for many documents is simply that information be transferred to and stored for the **AUDIENCE**. The **OBJECTIVE** then is to convey this information as clearly as possible.

POWERFUL WRITTEN DOCUMENTS

THOUGHTFUL ORGANIZATION
Written documents can quickly become dense with information and appear overwhelming to read. By taking time to organize and present the information from most to least important, you greatly increase the likelihood that your message will be clear and understood. Remember the BLUF strategy: Bottom Line Up Front.

CLEAR HIERARCHY
Include headlines and distinct titles for topics to give your audience a quick reference to what they can expect from each section. Well-crafted titles and headlines can convey the bulk of your message to your audience from simply scanning these. These mile-markers in your text allow your audience to quickly focus on what is important to them.

FEWER WORDS. MORE IMPACT.
Practice conveying your message with as few words as possible to dramatically elevate their importance to the reader.

HEXXIS GAME TESTING

Focus Group Report

April 26, 2016 | Laura Judge

SUMMARY

10 casual gamers were asked to play HEXXIS for 30 minutes each, then interviewed as a group about their gameplay experience. The resounding response was extremely positive.

> 8 of the 10 players were willing to purchase the game for $3.99.
> 6 players knew friends or family that they thought would like the game
> All of the players were able to complete the first level within 90 seconds
> 5 of the players were willing to pay 99¢ to upgrade to the Pro version

INTERVIEW HIGHLIGHTS

"The graphics are very cool. It looks very simple but it quickly gets difficult - which makes for a fun challenge."

"I found myself humming the songs for each level. I'd love to get the soundtrack."

"If I could play against my friends in real-time - that would be amazing."

"It's like Tetris meets Words with Friends. Simple but complicated at the same time."

TOP CONCERNS

3 areas of concern were mentioned by multiple players. These represent opportunities for improvement ahead of the final release:

> The power-up was hard to find - needs to be more obvious
> The level scoring did not make sense to most players.
> The level speeds increase too fast. A more gradual change will help

A detailed report will follow.

###

POWERFUL DATA DOCUMENTS

IT'S ABOUT THE NUMBERS, NOT THE CELLS
Most spreadsheets are presented in a grid, with the data competing for attention with the cell frames. While the grid is helpful for organizing, it can be very distracting when reading the data. Hide the grid and let the data create the structure for the columns and rows.

USE SIZE & WEIGHT FOR EMPHASIS
Data that should be highlighted for your viewer can be emphasized by changing the weight, size or color of the numbers. Adjusting the numbers themselves in place of coloring the cell, keeps the focus on the data.

HIDE ANCILLARY DATA
While a complex and dense amount of data may be needed to calculate your results, only some of that data is necessary for your audience to understand the conclusions. Hide as much data as possible that is not relevant to the message you want to convey. This information will still be available if needed but not distracting your audience from the key message.

HEXXIS GAME BUDGET

	BUDGET	ACTUAL	DIFFERENCE
DESIGN	$ 150,000	$ 197,000	$ (47,000)
Game Design	$ 100,000	$ 144,000	
Web Design	$ 25,000	$ 22,000	
Marketing Design	$ 25,000	$ 31,000	
DEVELOPMENT	$ 700,000	$ 823,000	$ (123,000)
iOS Dev	$ 300,000	$ 410,000	
Android Dev	$ 350,000	$ 325,000	
Back-End Dev	$ 50,000	$ 88,000	
QA / TESTING	$ 130,000	$ 98,000	$ 32,000
iOS QA	$ 50,000	$ 40,000	
Android QA	$ 60,000	$ 35,000	
Logic Testing	$ 20,000	$ 23,000	
MARKETING	$ 270,000	$ 212,000	$ 58,000
US Marketing	$ 80,000	$ 40,000	
European Marketing	$ 80,000	$ 60,000	
Japan Marketing	$ 60,000	$ 42,000	
Other Marketing	$ 50,000	$ 70,000	
OVERHEAD	$ 750,000	$ 795,000	$ (45,000)
Admin Salaries	$ 245,000	$ 220,000	
Support Salaries	$ 165,000	$ 190,000	
Studio - Boulder	$ 190,000	$ 205,000	
Studio - Hyderabad	$ 85,000	$ 70,000	
Operations	$ 65,000	$ 110,000	
TOTALS	**$2,000,000**	**$ 2,125,000**	**$(125,000)**

POWERFUL VISUAL DOCUMENTS

CHARTS ARE IMAGES

Whenever possible, use a chart or graph to illustrate data analysis and results. A powerful chart is worth a thousand data points.

IMAGES CREATE FEELINGS

Use images in documents to convey concepts. Images can express ideas quickly and leave a lasting impression. Use images that are intriguing and unexpected to make an even stronger impression.

AVOID CLICHÉS

Using traditional clip-art or common stock photography images can work against your intent. These types of images have become expected and so common-place that they suggest that your message is unoriginal. Look for new ways to express concepts to create original connections for your audience.

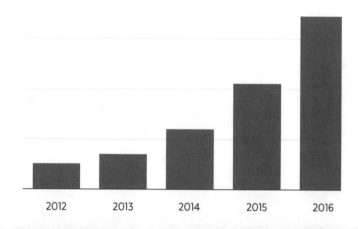

OUR MARKET

Millions of Mobile Gamers

2012   2013   2014   2015   2016

HEXXIS.   elegant complexity

POWERFUL STORY DOCUMENTS

STORYTELLING

Telling stories is one of the most effective ways to make a strong impact on your audience. A good story will have a start, middle and end that takes your audience on a trip that they can relate to. When you can tell a story that connects with your audience, you give your ideas the best chance of staying with them.

FROM DECKS TO STORYBOOKS

Instead of assembling a series of slides, consider creating a storybook. By outlining the story you want to share, each page can then focus on moving the story forward. When you can tell the story in person to your audience, the pages become the illustrations to your tale. Aspire to moving your audience with your imagination and delivery.

Beginning

Middle

End

COLLABORATING ON DOCUMENTS

Collaborating on documents with a team requires a conscious effort to streamline the process. The first step is to understand and agree on the process in advance. With a transparent process and approach, everyone participating can stay focused on what they are contributing.

COLLABORATION WORKFLOW

1 OUTLINE
An outline of the document is created and agreed upon.

2 WRITTEN DRAFT
An initial draft of the content in text is crafted for comment.

3 FINAL CONTENT
A final version of the text and additional content is accepted.

4 LAYOUT
The document is formatted and designed.

5 REVIEW
The document is reviewed, edited and approved.

6 DISTRIBUTION
A final version is created for distribution as a PDF.

ONE VERSION TO RULE THEM ALL

The advent of cloud storage solutions has made it convenient and simple to collaborate on documents across teams, no matter where in the world each member might be. Instead of the old-fashioned method of creating versions, distributing those versions and reconciling comments from each individual, a single, central document is used. Most modern software incorporates automatic version history and change-tracking, allowing a single document to be saved in the cloud and worked on collaboratively without need for distributing copies.

SHARING FINISHED DOCUMENTS

When documents are finalized, it's important to freeze them in their final form so further changes are not made unintentionally. These final versions are then ready for sharing and distribution with confidence that everyone will be seeing the same version.

THE PDF IS FOR EVERYONE

The Portable Document Format (PDF) was designed to allow documents to be saved and shared in a format that ensures everyone will see the exact same thing. The PDF eliminates issues with how documents appear on different platforms, where different fonts, screen resolutions and other factors can make native document files appear differently. PDFs are generally unable to be edited or changed, making this format ideal for packaging all final document versions. All modern document creation software includes an option to save a PDF of your documents.

DOCUMENT SECURITY

Another important reason to only distribute final documents in PDF format is for security. If we distribute final documents in native formats (Word, Excel or PowerPoint) these documents can be easily edited and changed in ways that can confuse or disrupt the original intent. For example, sending a 3-page non-disclosure agreement to a partner in an editable format could allow for subtle changes to be made and never noticed when the signed document is returned.

Avoid the potential for unintended changes by sharing only PDFs which are not easily edited.

DISTRIBUTING

Cloud storage platforms also make it convenient and efficient to distribute these PDFs. Instead of sending copies throughout your network, share a link to the document stored in the cloud where anyone can access and view it without needing to make a local copy of their own. With this approach, updating the document becomes as easy as updating the file in the cloud, and anyone with access to it will immediately have the new version available.

ALWAYS DISTRIBUTE FINAL DOCUMENTS IN PDF FORMAT.

PDFs ensure the content of your document is not easily changed and allows anyone to open the document on any device.

ALL DOCUMENTS BEGIN AS A WRITTEN OUTLINE.

A written outline is the most efficient way to define your objectives, audience, message and actions. Refinement and agreement on the outline make the process of creating any document smoother.

FUNDAMENTALS FOR

PRESENTATIONS

Ted hadn't had much time to prepare for his pre-sentation — but he didn't let that shake his confi-dence. Besides, if he forgot what he wanted to say it was up there word-for-word on his slides.

Amy was frantic — she was only halfway through her slides with 5-minutes to go. Where had the time gone?

"We'll get back to you," said the client, stifling a yawn. Joan knew what that meant. But she didn't understand what they could have done differently — everything had been described in such detail on their 80-slide deck.

Have you ever listened to a presentation like this?

Have you ever given a presentation like this?

STREAMLINING PRESENTATIONS

MAKE AN IMPACT

The act of sharing information can become an art form when we invest in our presentation. Whether we are sharing a gift or information, it is important to set the stage for our audience — signal to them that we believe we have something special to give.

When we believe what we are sharing is unique and valuable, our presentation should reflect this as well.

UNDERSTANDING PRESENTATIONS

TALKS

When an individual presents a talk, they are typically making an address to an audience without feedback from or engagement with the audience. Talks are primarily one-way sharing. Modern talks (like TED talks or a keynote address) often include slides that can be powerful tools for the presenter.

MEETINGS

Meetings often include presentations in which information is shared and discussions take place. For these, the presentation serves as the outline for the discussion, which is expected to be engaging and collaborative. Modern meeting and conference rooms are designed to facilitate these presentation-led gatherings.

CONVERSATIONS

Presentations have even found their way into one-on-one conversations, where slides become cue-cards designed to drive the discussion. Pitching an idea to a person in today's business environment has become synonymous with presenting a slide deck instead of a simple discussion.

All three types of presentation share some things in common:

The speaker and audience are in the same place together.
The slides serve to support what the speaker is saying.
The speaker is responsible for dynamically presenting the
message - not the slides.

A PRESENTATION THAT IS NOT PRESENTED IS JUST A DOCUMENT.

The act of creating a presentation has been confused with the art of presenting. The success of any presentation lies with the speaker's ability to connect the information to the audience. When we remove this dynamic, the chance of making an impact is severely compromised.

COMPROMISE
Unfortunately, it has become increasingly common to forgo this connection in the interest of distributing ideas on their own and without the context a presenter provides. This has led to the creation of "presentations" that are never truly presented, only shared.

A DOCUMENT

> Exciting new model
> Best convertible we've ever built
> Maintains 4-star safety rating
> Over 225 improvements
> Just one highlight:
> Top down in 17 seconds!
> Full specs in your handout

FUEL ECONOMY (CTY/HWY)	11/20 mpg
CAR TYPE	Coupe
TRANSMISSION	6-speed Manual
BASIC WARRANTY	4 Yr./ 50000 Mi.
BLUETOOTH	Yes
HEATED SEATS	Yes
ENGINE TYPE	Gas
TOTAL SEATING	2
CYLINDERS	V8
DRIVE TRAIN	All Wheel Drive
CONSUMER RATING	Not Available
NAVIGATION	No

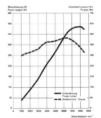

What's New for 2015

The 2015 Audi R8 gets two new trim levels called the V10 Carbon Spyder and the limited-edition 570-horsepower V10 Competition Coupe. There are also a few equipment changes including standard power-folding exterior mirrors on base models and an optional sport exhaust on V10 S tronic models.

Focuses on details.

A SLIDE

LESS IS MORE.

Focuses on the story.

ANATOMY OF A PRESENTATION

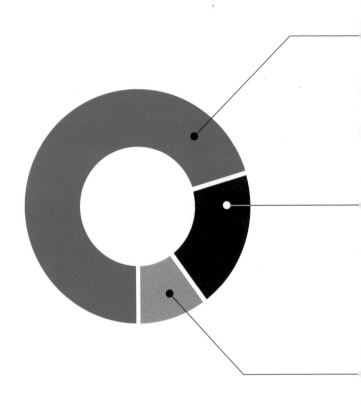

70% WHAT WE SAY

The most memorable part of our presentation is what we say and how we say it.
Our ability to explain details and make a
connection to our ideas cannot be
captured on a slide.

20% WHAT WE SHOW

Our slide serves to support what we say by
anchoring the audience's attention on a
single big idea. Powerful visuals and bold
statements reinforce the importance of
our key message.

10% WHAT WE SHARE

Providing your audience with details and
supporting information is best handled in a
format they can take with them or annotate.
Providing notes to your audience insures
everyone leaves with the same message.

WHAT WE SAY: BEST PRACTICES

NOTES, NOT A SCRIPT
Creating speaker notes for yourself will give you the sequence and highlights you want to include with each slide. Never try to write a script or exact wording for sentences. Always rely on your natural and personal delivery style based on your notes alone.

LISTEN TO CONNECT
When you listen and pay attention to your audience, you can get a sense of what is connecting and what is not. Where there is uncertainty, you can add more depth or try a different approach. When things are resonating, you can move on with confidence.

ENGAGE & INTERACT
Whenever you can interact with your audience — asking questions, looking for agreement or feedback — you draw them into the ideas. The less of a barrier you create between you and your audience, the less of a barrier there will be to your ideas.

SUNLIGHT IN **17** SECONDS

AUDI R8 SPIDER

> Exciting new model
> Best convertible we've ever built
> Maintains 4-star safety rating
> Over 225 improvements
> Just one highlight:
> Top down in 17 seconds!
> Full specs in your handout

Slide + speaker notes

WHAT WE SHOW: BEST PRACTICES

FOCUS ON THE KEY CONCEPT

A powerful slide makes the key concept or point you are making obvious and clear. Your audience should not have to parse or interpret exactly what the message and take-away is. You simply show it.

STRONG IMAGERY

Strong, effective images can create connections and generate feelings in your audience far easier than any words you can write. Whether you use graphs, illustrations or photos, one per page makes the strongest impression.

MINIMAL TEXT

Less words make more impact. Aim for no more than 15 words total on any one slide. Also avoid sentences which your audience will feel compelled to read. Use simple phrases or individual words to ensure your audience will be listening to what you say and not reading your slides.

SUNLIGHT IN SECONDS

LIKE A GLOVE.

WHAT WE SHARE: BEST PRACTICES

NOT THE SLIDE DECK
If your slides were created with the appropriate amount of content, they will have little value without you presenting them. Instead, create a separate document with notes to accompany the deck which can stand on its own.

PROVIDE DEPTH & DETAIL
Along with the notes, your document can provide further depth in areas you could not cover in person as well as specifics that were not presented. This extra information builds on the message you shared by giving further context for moving your ideas forward.

FOR REFERENCE
Your document becomes a reference which stands on its own. Your message, information and support are all self-contained and can be shared and reviewed without you presenting it. Taken together with what you show and say in your presentation, you will deliver a more powerful message.

5,2 Liter V10 FSI im Audi R8

mit FSI®. Benzindirekteinspritzung, kontinuierlicher Nockenwellenverstellung,
und Nockenwellenantrieb per Kette

5.2 litre V10 FSI engine in the Audi R8 with FSI®. Fuel direct injection, variable
camshaft timing and chain driven camshafts

5.204 cm³	5.204 cc
386 kW (525 PS) bei 8.000 min⁻¹	386 kW (525 bhp) at 8,000 rpm
530 Nm bei 6.500 min⁻¹	530 Nm at to 6,500 rpm

12/08

FUEL ECONOMY (CTY/HWY)	11/20 mpg
CAR TYPE	**Coupe**
TRANSMISSION	**6-speed Manual**
BASIC WARRANTY	**4 Yr./ 50000 Mi.**
BLUETOOTH	**Yes**
HEATED SEATS	**Yes**
ENGINE TYPE	**Gas**
TOTAL SEATING	**2**
CYLINDERS	**V8**
DRIVE TRAIN	**All Wheel Drive**
CONSUMER RATING	**Not Available**
NAVIGATION	**No**

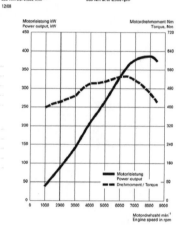

What's New for 2015

The 2015 Audi R8 gets two new trim levels called the V10 Carbon Spyder and the limited-edition
570-horsepower V10 Competition Coupe. There are also a few equipment changes including standard
power-folding exterior mirrors on base models and an optional sport exhaust on V10 S tronic models.

A COMPLETE PRESENTATION SUITE

SAY

Your speaker notes + your delivery

SHOW

Powerful slides, each with a single key message

SHARE

Your support document, providing notes to your audience.

LESS IS MORE.

LIKE A GLOVE.

Slides

AUDI R8 SPIDER

> Exciting new model
> Best convertible we've ever built
> Maintains 4-star safety rating
> Over 225 improvements
> Just one highlight:
> Top down in 17 seconds!
> Full specs in your handout

Speaker notes

Handout

WITHOUT A PRESENTER, A PRESENTATION TELLS A POOR STORY.

A good presentation includes the imagery and essence of your story, with your words filling in the details. A presentation sent on its own only carries a fraction of the message.

USE STATEMENTS NOT SENTENCES TO KEEP YOUR MESSAGE CONCISE.

When you present, you speak and share in full sentences. The slides are summaries of the concepts, not a script.

USE AS FEW SLIDES AS POSSIBLE. LESS SLIDES CREATE MORE ATTENTION.

Take 100 and divide by your number of slides to calculate the percentage of attention each slide will receive. 5 slides means each get 20%. 50 slides...only 2%.

SLIDES SHOULD ILLUSTRATE WHAT YOU ARE SAYING.

Powerful slides illustrate and summarize the most important point you are making. They are your backup band while you are the star.

THE WAY

FOCUSED COMMUNICATION

The principles of Focused Communication and Streamlining all lead us to the same place.

THE LESS COMPLEX OUR COMMUNICATION, THE MORE POWERFUL OUR MESSAGE.

Where **MORE** is the common route,
LESS is the more elegant way.

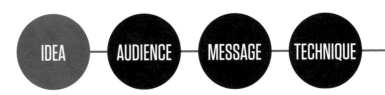

Taking this road less traveled, our compass keeps us focused on our destination

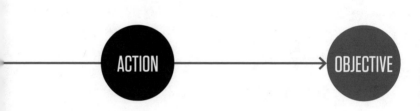

The success of
communication can
only be measured
by the impact it makes.

After everything is
said & done,
when less is said,
more is done.

GLOSSARY

BLUF
BOTTOM LINE UP FRONT

A reminder to always lead communication with the most relevant conclusion or decision.

BTT
BACK TO TOPIC

A helpful guidepost for messages and threads that have strayed from their original intent.

COB
CLOSE OF BUSINESS

Sometimes interchnaged with EOD (End of Day), this acronym relates the concept of timing without needing to specify a time in our world of distributed teams.

EOM
END OF MESSAGE

A simple courtesy to indicate the completion of a message - typically appended to short messages so there is no confusion by the audience that the brief message is complete.

NNTR

NO NEED TO REPLY

A courtesy indication that the writer is not expecting a reply. NNTR is a powerful way to end reply loops and avoid unnecessary confirmations.

TL;DR

TOO LONG; DIDN'T READ

Sometimes pronounced "teal deer", this notation informs the sender that the reader found the content too dense and she did not spend the time to parse it for the intended message.

TS;DU

TOO SHORT; DIDN'T UNDERSTAND

The counterpoint to TL;DR, this notation informs the sender that more context or clarity is needed to fully understand the message.

THE AUTHORS

JASON FRANZEN
Co-Founder of Streamline Certified
StreamlineCertified.com

Founder of More Simple
MoreSimple.com

STEPHAN MARDYKS
Co-Founder of Streamline Certified
StreamlineCertified.com

Co-CEO & Co-Founder of SMCOV
SMCOV.com

Managing Partner of ThomasLeland
ThomasLeland.com

SINCERE APPRECIATION

Heartfelt thanks to our wives Laura and Marie-Genet
and our families for their continual support of our passion
for streamlining.

Special thanks to David MR Covey, Joseph Alan Wachs and
David Wesley Covey for their thoughtful contributions.

Our admiration to David Allen for inspiring us
and for his foreword to our book.

And of course to Stephen R. Covey for reminding us to keep
the main thing the main thing when interacting with others.

COLOPHON

DESIGN

Book design and layout by Jason Alan Franzen

This book is set in Texta type from Latinotype foundry and Tungsten type from Hoefler & Co.

Photos are from the Shutterstock library and the author's collection.

STREAMLINE CERTIFIED TRAINING

Streamline Certified offers a suite of training programs for in-person and on-line adoption of streamlining principles and best practices.

FOR LEADERS

Streamlined Leadership training introduces the power of a culture of streamlined communication in organizations.

FOR INDIVIDUALS

Streamlined Communication training teaches the art and power of streamlining for today's emerging talent.

To learn more about incorporating Focused Communication in yours or your organization's communication plan, visit:

StreamlineCertified.com

Art   Power   Culture

Why   How   Who

The Streamlined trilogy offers a continuum of insight and application of the principles of focus and simplicity in modern communication.

LESS & MORE
THE ART OF SAYING MORE WITH LESS

SAID & DONE
THE POWER OF SAYING MORE WITH LESS

LESS SAID. MORE DONE.
CHAMPIONING A CULTURE OF
STREAMLINED COMMUNICATION

Complete your collection or share a book
with your colleagues at StreamlineCertified.com

The simplest things are often the truest.

– RICHARD BACH